THIS IEP PLANNER

Belongs To

VERSION 2

BY SPED DEV PUBLISHING

ANY QUESTION ?
CONTACT US AT
Speddevpublishing@gmail.com

Our Website : iepplanners.com

Table Of Content

⯈⯈⯈ Teacher
Info

Contact

Name   :

Phone   :

School :

Email   :

City   :

Address :

District :

Classes

CLASS	NUMBER OF STUDENTS	ROOM

>>> School Timetable <<<

TIME						
MONDAY						
TUESDAY						
WEDNESDAY						
THURSDAY						
FRIDAY						

Notes :

....

....

....

....

....

Additional info

▸▸▸ Important Info

Online File Storage

(FILES - VIDEOS - PHOTOS...)

TITLE	LINK	PASSWORD

Email Accounts

EMAIL	PASSWORD

Other Passwords

WEBSITE	USERNAME	PASSWORD

▶▶▶ Useful Contacts
Info

Useful Contacts

Name
....

Address
....

....

Phone
....

Fax
....

Email
....

Addit Info
....

....

Name
....

Address
....

....

Phone
....

Fax
....

Email
....

Addit Info
....

....

Name
....

Address
....

....

Phone
....

Fax
....

Email
....

Addit Info
....

....

Name
....

Address
....

....

Phone
....

Fax
....

Email
....

Addit Info
....

....

Name
....

Address
....

....

Phone
....

Fax
....

Email
....

Addit Info
....

....

Name
....

Address
....

....

Phone
....

Fax
....

Email
....

Addit Info
....

....

Name
....

Address
....

....

Phone
....

Fax
....

Email
....

Addit Info
....

....

Name
....

Address
....

....

Phone
....

Fax
....

Email
....

Addit Info
....

....

Name
....

Address
....

....

Phone
....

Fax
....

Email
....

Addit Info
....

....

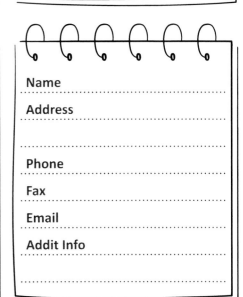

Useful Contacts

Name ....
Address ....
....
Phone ....
Fax ....
Email ....
Addit Info ....
....

Name ....
Address ....
....
Phone ....
Fax ....
Email ....
Addit Info ....
....

Name ....
Address ....
....
Phone ....
Fax ....
Email ....
Addit Info ....
....

Name ....
Address ....
....
Phone ....
Fax ....
Email ....
Addit Info ....
....

Name ....
Address ....
....
Phone ....
Fax ....
Email ....
Addit Info ....
....

Name ....
Address ....
....
Phone ....
Fax ....
Email ....
Addit Info ....
....

Name ....
Address ....
....
Phone ....
Fax ....
Email ....
Addit Info ....
....

Name ....
Address ....
....
Phone ....
Fax ....
Email ....
Addit Info ....
....

Name ....
Address ....
....
Phone ....
Fax ....
Email ....
Addit Info ....
....

Useful Contacts

Name

Address

Phone

Fax

Email

Addit Info

Name

Address

Phone

Fax

Email

Addit Info

Name

Address

Phone

Fax

Email

Addit Info

Name

Address

Phone

Fax

Email

Addit Info

Name

Address

Phone

Fax

Email

Addit Info

Name

Address

Phone

Fax

Email

Addit Info

Name

Address

Phone

Fax

Email

Addit Info

Name

Address

Phone

Fax

Email

Addit Info

Name

Address

Phone

Fax

Email

Addit Info

►►►Iep Meetings
Calendar

IEP Meetings
Calendar

Aug

TITLE	DUE DATE

Sep

TITLE	DUE DATE

Oct

TITLE	DUE DATE

Nov

TITLE	DUE DATE

IEP Meetings
Calendar

Dec

TITLE	DUE DATE

Jan

TITLE	DUE DATE

Feb

TITLE	DUE DATE

Mar

TITLE	DUE DATE

IEP Meetings
Calendar

Apr

TITLE	DUE DATE

May

TITLE	DUE DATE

Jun

TITLE	DUE DATE

Jul

TITLE	DUE DATE

⯈⯈⯈Iep Caseload

IEP Caseload
Info

NUMBER	STUDENT'S NAME	ID #	GRADE	DATE OF BIRTH	IEP EXPIRATION DATE

IEP Caseload Info

#	STUDENT'S NAME	ID #	GRADE	DATE OF BIRTH	IEP EXPIRATION DATE

▶▶▶ Student's Name ◀◀◀

ID .... Grade ....

Number

Student info

Student's Name		Student ID	
Date Of Birth		Grade	
IEP Expiration Date		ETR Expiration Date	

❤ Contact Info ❤

Name		Name	
Relationship		Relationship	
Phone Number		Phone Number	
Email		Email	

❤ IEP GOALS ❤

		Related Services ❤	Time
	☐	Occupational Therapy	
	☐	Physical Therapy	
	☐	Speech Therapy	
	☐	Behavioral Therapy	
	☐	Other :	

❤ Important Information ❤

Medication	Other

IEP Snapshot

Student's Name: _____ Case Manager: _____ Date of IEP: _____

Disability: _____ Eligibility: _____ Behavior Plan: ☐ **Yes** ☐ **No**

ⅴ Subject ⅴ	ⅴ Goal ⅴ

ⅴ Accommodations ⅴ

IN THE CLASSROOM	TESTING

ⅴ Strengths ⅴ	ⅴ Need To Know ⅴ

ⅴ Weaknesses ⅴ	ⅴ Notes ⅴ

IEP Meeting Checklist

Student's Name		IEP Due Date	
Date Of Birth		Classification	
Grade		Meeting Date	

⌄ Before Meeting ⌄

⌄ Day of Meeting ⌄

⌄ After Meeting ⌄

>>> IEP Meeting Notes <<<

Student's Name		**IEP Due Date**	
Date Of Birth		**Classification**	
Grade		**Meeting Date**	

Attendees ☐ **Parent/Guardian**   ☐ **OT**   ☐ **PT**   Meeting Purpose ....

☐ **Classroom Teacher**   ☐ **Speech**   ....

☐ **Other** ....

....

❣ Parent Concerns ❣

❣ Student's Progress ❣

❣ Next Steps ❣

▶▶▶ Progress Monitoring

Progress Monitoring

Student's Name : ....   Grade : ....

Goals	
1	**2**
3	**4**
5	**6**

Goal #	Date	Trial 1	Date	Trial 2	Date	Trial 3

ᵛ Comments ᵛ

⠒⠒ Progress Monitoring ⠶⠶

Student's Name : ....   Grade : ....

Goals	
1	**2** ....
3	**4** ....
5	**6** ....

Goal #	Date	Trial 1	Date	Trial 2	Date	Trial 3

⌵ Comments ⌵

....

....

....

....

....

Small Group Progress Monitoring

Subject : ....   Week of : ....

Date	Target Skill and Activity	Students	Notes

Communication Log

MOTHER		FATHER		OTHER CONTACT	
Email		Email		Email	
Cell		Cell		Cell	
Work		Work		Work	

DATE & TIME	TO	METHOD OF CONTACT	REASON FOR CONTACT	FOLLOW UP	NOTES
		☐ Call ☐ Email ☐ Note ☐ Meeting ☐ Other:		☐ YES ☐ NO	
		☐ Call ☐ Email ☐ Note ☐ Meeting ☐ Other:		☐ YES ☐ NO	
		☐ Call ☐ Email ☐ Note ☐ Meeting ☐ Other:		☐ YES ☐ NO	
		☐ Call ☐ Email ☐ Note ☐ Meeting ☐ Other:		☐ YES ☐ NO	
		☐ Call ☐ Email ☐ Note ☐ Meeting ☐ Other:		☐ YES ☐ NO	
		☐ Call ☐ Email ☐ Note ☐ Meeting ☐ Other:		☐ YES ☐ NO	

>>> Communication Log <<<

DATE & TIME	TO	METHOD OF CONTACT	REASON FOR CONTACT	FOLLOW UP	NOTES
		☐ Call ☐ Email ☐ Note ☐ Meeting ☐ Other:		☐ YES ☐ NO	
		☐ Call ☐ Email ☐ Note ☐ Meeting ☐ Other:		☐ YES ☐ NO	
		☐ Call ☐ Email ☐ Note ☐ Meeting ☐ Other:		☐ YES ☐ NO	
		☐ Call ☐ Email ☐ Note ☐ Meeting ☐ Other:		☐ YES ☐ NO	
		☐ Call ☐ Email ☐ Note ☐ Meeting ☐ Other:		☐ YES ☐ NO	
		☐ Call ☐ Email ☐ Note ☐ Meeting ☐ Other:		☐ YES ☐ NO	
		☐ Call ☐ Email ☐ Note ☐ Meeting ☐ Other:		☐ YES ☐ NO	
		☐ Call ☐ Email ☐ Note ☐ Meeting ☐ Other:		☐ YES ☐ NO	

Observations

Date :

Date :

Date :

Date :

Date :

Date :

Date :

Date :

Date :

Observations

Date :

Date :

Date :

Date :

Date :

Date :

Date :

Date :

Date :

▶▶▶ Student's Name ◀◀◀

ID .... Grade ....

Number

Student Info

Student's Name		Student ID	
Date Of Birth		Grade	
IEP Expiration Date		ETR Expiration Date	

⌣ Contact Info ⌣

Name		Name	
Relationship		Relationship	
Phone Number		Phone Number	
Email		Email	

⌣ IEP GOALS ⌣

⌣ Related Services ⌣	Time
☐ Occupational Therapy	
☐ Physical Therapy	
☐ Speech Therapy	
☐ Behavioral Therapy	
☐ Other :	

⌣ Important Information ⌣	
Medication	Other

IEP Snapshot

Student's Name: _____ Case Manager: _____ Date of IEP: _____

Disability: _____ Eligibility: _____ Behavior Plan: ☐ Yes ☐ No

⌄ Subject ⌄

⌄ Goal ⌄

⌄ Accommodations ⌄

IN THE CLASSROOM	TESTING

⌄ Strengths ⌄

⌄ Need To Know ⌄

⌄ Weaknesses ⌄

⌄ Notes ⌄

IEP Meeting Checklist

Student's Name		IEP Due Date	
Date Of Birth		Classification	
Grade		Meeting Date	

Before Meeting

Day of Meeting

After Meeting

IEP Meeting Notes

Student's Name		**IEP Due Date**	
Date Of Birth		**Classification**	
Grade		**Meeting Date**	

Attendees
☐ Parent/Guardian   ☐ OT   ☐ PT
☐ Classroom Teacher   ☐ Speech
☐ Other

Meeting Purpose
....
....
....

❤ Parent Concerns ❤

❤ Student's Progress ❤

❤ Next Steps ❤

Progress Monitoring

Progress Monitoring

Student's Name : ....   Grade : ....

Goals			
1		2	
3		4	
5		6	

Goal #	Date	Trial 1	Date	Trial 2	Date	Trial 3

Comments

Progress Monitoring

Student's Name : ....   Grade : ....

Goals			
1		2	
3		4	
5		6	

Goal #	Date	Trial 1	Date	Trial 2	Date	Trial 3

⩔ Comments ⩔

Small Group Progress
Monitoring

Subject : ....   Week of : ....

Date	Target Skill and Activity	Students	Notes

>>> Communication Log <<<

MOTHER		FATHER		OTHER CONTACT	
Email		Email		Email	
Cell		Cell		Cell	
Work		Work		Work	

DATE & TIME	TO	METHOD OF CONTACT	REASON FOR CONTACT	FOLLOW UP	NOTES
		☐ Call ☐ Email ☐ Note ☐ Meeting ☐ Other:		☐ YES ☐ NO	
		☐ Call ☐ Email ☐ Note ☐ Meeting ☐ Other:		☐ YES ☐ NO	
		☐ Call ☐ Email ☐ Note ☐ Meeting ☐ Other:		☐ YES ☐ NO	
		☐ Call ☐ Email ☐ Note ☐ Meeting ☐ Other:		☐ YES ☐ NO	
		☐ Call ☐ Email ☐ Note ☐ Meeting ☐ Other:		☐ YES ☐ NO	
		☐ Call ☐ Email ☐ Note ☐ Meeting ☐ Other:		☐ YES ☐ NO	

>>> Communication Log <<<

DATE & TIME	TO	METHOD OF CONTACT	REASON FOR CONTACT	FOLLOW UP	NOTES
		☐ Call ☐ Email ☐ Note ☐ Meeting ☐ Other:		☐ YES ☐ NO	
		☐ Call ☐ Email ☐ Note ☐ Meeting ☐ Other:		☐ YES ☐ NO	
		☐ Call ☐ Email ☐ Note ☐ Meeting ☐ Other:		☐ YES ☐ NO	
		☐ Call ☐ Email ☐ Note ☐ Meeting ☐ Other:		☐ YES ☐ NO	
		☐ Call ☐ Email ☐ Note ☐ Meeting ☐ Other:		☐ YES ☐ NO	
		☐ Call ☐ Email ☐ Note ☐ Meeting ☐ Other:		☐ YES ☐ NO	
		☐ Call ☐ Email ☐ Note ☐ Meeting ☐ Other:		☐ YES ☐ NO	
		☐ Call ☐ Email ☐ Note ☐ Meeting ☐ Other:		☐ YES ☐ NO	

Observations

Date :

Date :

Date :

Date :

Date :

Date :

Date :

Date :

Date :

Observations

| Date : | Date : | Date : |

| Date : | Date : | Date : |

| Date : | Date : | Date : |

▶▶▶ Student's Name ◀◀◀

ID .... Grade ....

Number

Student info

Student's Name	Student ID
Date Of Birth	Grade
IEP Expiration Date	ETR Expiration Date

♥ Contact Info ♥

Name	Name
Relationship	Relationship
Phone Number	Phone Number
Email	Email

♥ IEP GOALS ♥

♥ Related Services ♥	Time
☐ Occupational Therapy	
☐ Physical Therapy	
☐ Speech Therapy	
☐ Behavioral Therapy	
☐ Other :	

♥ Important Information ♥

Medication	Other

IEP Snapshot

Student's Name: [ ] Case Manager: [ ] Date of IEP: [ ]

Disability: [ ] Eligibility: [ ] Behavior Plan: [ ] **Yes** [ ] **No**

❥ Subject ❥	❥ Goal ❥

❥ Accommodations ❥

IN THE CLASSROOM	TESTING

❥ Strengths ❥	❥ Need To Know ❥

❥ Weaknesses ❥	❥ Notes ❥

IEP Meeting Checklist

Student's Name		IEP Due Date	
Date Of Birth		Classification	
Grade		Meeting Date	

⌵ Before Meeting ⌵

⌵ Day of Meeting ⌵

⌵ After Meeting ⌵

IEP Meeting Notes

Student's Name	**IEP Due Date**
Date Of Birth	**Classification**
Grade	**Meeting Date**

Attendees   ☐ Parent/Guardian   ☐ OT   ☐ PT

☐ Classroom Teacher   ☐ Speech

☐ Other

Meeting Purpose ....

....

....

❣ Parent Concerns ❣

❣ Student's Progress ❣

❣ Next Steps ❣

▶▶▶ Progress Monitoring

Progress Monitoring

Student's Name : .... 　Grade : ....

Goals			
1		2	
3		4	
5		6	

Goal #	Date	Trial 1	Date	Trial 2	Date	Trial 3

⌄ Comments ⌄

Progress Monitoring

Student's Name : .... Grade : ....

Goals			
1		**2**	
3		**4**	
5		**6**	

Goal #	Date	Trial 1	Date	Trial 2	Date	Trial 3

∨ Comments ∨

Small Group Progress
Monitoring

Subject : .... 　　 Week of : ....

Date	Target Skill and Activity	Students	Notes

Communication Log

MOTHER	FATHER	OTHER CONTACT
Email	Email	Email
Cell	Cell	Cell
Work	Work	Work

DATE & TIME	TO	METHOD OF CONTACT	REASON FOR CONTACT	FOLLOW UP	NOTES
		☐ Call ☐ Email ☐ Note ☐ Meeting ☐ Other:		☐ YES ☐ NO	
		☐ Call ☐ Email ☐ Note ☐ Meeting ☐ Other:		☐ YES ☐ NO	
		☐ Call ☐ Email ☐ Note ☐ Meeting ☐ Other:		☐ YES ☐ NO	
		☐ Call ☐ Email ☐ Note ☐ Meeting ☐ Other:		☐ YES ☐ NO	
		☐ Call ☐ Email ☐ Note ☐ Meeting ☐ Other:		☐ YES ☐ NO	
		☐ Call ☐ Email ☐ Note ☐ Meeting ☐ Other:		☐ YES ☐ NO	

Communication Log

DATE & TIME	TO	METHOD OF CONTACT	REASON FOR CONTACT	FOLLOW UP	NOTES
		☐ Call ☐ Email ☐ Note ☐ Meeting ☐ Other:		☐ YES ☐ NO	
		☐ Call ☐ Email ☐ Note ☐ Meeting ☐ Other:		☐ YES ☐ NO	
		☐ Call ☐ Email ☐ Note ☐ Meeting ☐ Other:		☐ YES ☐ NO	
		☐ Call ☐ Email ☐ Note ☐ Meeting ☐ Other:		☐ YES ☐ NO	
		☐ Call ☐ Email ☐ Note ☐ Meeting ☐ Other:		☐ YES ☐ NO	
		☐ Call ☐ Email ☐ Note ☐ Meeting ☐ Other:		☐ YES ☐ NO	
		☐ Call ☐ Email ☐ Note ☐ Meeting ☐ Other:		☐ YES ☐ NO	
		☐ Call ☐ Email ☐ Note ☐ Meeting ☐ Other:		☐ YES ☐ NO	

Observations

Date :

Date :

Date :

Date :

Date :

Date :

Date :

Date :

Date :

Observations

Date :

Date :

Date :

Date :

Date :

Date :

Date :

Date :

Date :

▶▶▶ Student's Name ◀◀◀

ID ....   Grade ....

Number

Student info

Student's Name		Student ID	
Date Of Birth		Grade	
IEP Expiration Date		ETR Expiration Date	

♥ Contact Info ♥

Name		Name	
Relationship		Relationship	
Phone Number		Phone Number	
Email		Email	

♥ IEP GOALS ♥

♥ Related Services ♥	Time
☐ Occupational Therapy	
☐ Physical Therapy	
☐ Speech Therapy	
☐ Behavioral Therapy	
☐ Other :	

♥ Important Information ♥

Medication	Other

IEP Snapshot

Student's Name: _____ Case Manager: _____ Date of IEP: _____

Disability: _____ Eligibility: _____ Behavior Plan: ☐ Yes ☐ No

♥ Subject ♥

♥ Goal ♥

♥ Accommodations ♥

IN THE CLASSROOM	TESTING

♥ Strengths ♥

♥ Need To Know ♥

♥ Weaknesses ♥

♥ Notes ♥

IEP Meeting Checklist

Student's Name		IEP Due Date	
Date Of Birth		Classification	
Grade		Meeting Date	

❤ Before Meeting ❤

❤ Day of Meeting ❤

❤ After Meeting ❤

IEP Meeting Notes

Student's Name		IEP Due Date	
Date Of Birth		Classification	
Grade		Meeting Date	

Attendees
☐ Parent/Guardian   ☐ OT   ☐ PT
☐ Classroom Teacher   ☐ Speech
☐ Other

Meeting Purpose
....
....
....

❤ Parent Concerns ❤

❤ Student's Progress ❤

❤ Next Steps ❤

▸▸▸ Progress Monitoring

Progress Monitoring

Student's Name : ....   Grade : ....

Goals		
1		2
3		4
5		6

Goal #	Date	Trial 1	Date	Trial 2	Date	Trial 3

⌄ Comments ⌄

Progress Monitoring

Student's Name : ....   Grade : ....

Goals			
1		**2**	
3		**4**	
5		**6**	

Goal #	Date	Trial 1	Date	Trial 2	Date	Trial 3

⌄ Comments ⌄

Small Group Progress
Monitoring

Subject : ....   Week of : ....

Date	Target Skill and Activity	Students	Notes

⋙ Communication Log ⋘

MOTHER	FATHER	OTHER CONTACT
Email	Email	Email
Cell	Cell	Cell
Work	Work	Work

DATE & TIME	TO	METHOD OF CONTACT	REASON FOR CONTACT	FOLLOW UP	NOTES
		☐ Call ☐ Email ☐ Note ☐ Meeting ☐ Other:		☐ YES ☐ NO	
		☐ Call ☐ Email ☐ Note ☐ Meeting ☐ Other:		☐ YES ☐ NO	
		☐ Call ☐ Email ☐ Note ☐ Meeting ☐ Other:		☐ YES ☐ NO	
		☐ Call ☐ Email ☐ Note ☐ Meeting ☐ Other:		☐ YES ☐ NO	
		☐ Call ☐ Email ☐ Note ☐ Meeting ☐ Other:		☐ YES ☐ NO	
		☐ Call ☐ Email ☐ Note ☐ Meeting ☐ Other:		☐ YES ☐ NO	

≫≫ Communication Log ≪≪

DATE & TIME	TO	METHOD OF CONTACT	REASON FOR CONTACT	FOLLOW UP	NOTES
		☐ Call ☐ Email ☐ Note ☐ Meeting ☐ Other:		☐ YES ☐ NO	
		☐ Call ☐ Email ☐ Note ☐ Meeting ☐ Other:		☐ YES ☐ NO	
		☐ Call ☐ Email ☐ Note ☐ Meeting ☐ Other:		☐ YES ☐ NO	
		☐ Call ☐ Email ☐ Note ☐ Meeting ☐ Other:		☐ YES ☐ NO	
		☐ Call ☐ Email ☐ Note ☐ Meeting ☐ Other:		☐ YES ☐ NO	
		☐ Call ☐ Email ☐ Note ☐ Meeting ☐ Other:		☐ YES ☐ NO	
		☐ Call ☐ Email ☐ Note ☐ Meeting ☐ Other:		☐ YES ☐ NO	
		☐ Call ☐ Email ☐ Note ☐ Meeting ☐ Other:		☐ YES ☐ NO	

Observations

Date :

Date :

Date :

Date :

Date :

Date :

Date :

Date :

Date :

Observations

Date :

Date :

Date :

Date :

Date :

Date :

Date :

Date :

Date :

▶▶▶ Student's Name ◀◀◀

ID .... Grade ....

Number

Student info

Student's Name		Student ID	
Date Of Birth		Grade	
IEP Expiration Date		ETR Expiration Date	

❤ Contact Info ❤

Name		Name	
Relationship		Relationship	
Phone Number		Phone Number	
Email		Email	

❤ IEP GOALS ❤

❤ Related Services ❤	Time
☐ Occupational Therapy	
☐ Physical Therapy	
☐ Speech Therapy	
☐ Behavioral Therapy	
☐ Other :	

❤ Important Information ❤

Medication	Other

IEP Snapshot

Student's Name: _____ Case Manager: _____ Date of IEP: _____

Disability: _____ Eligibility: _____ Behavior Plan: ☐ **Yes** ☐ **No**

Subject	Goal

Accommodations

IN THE CLASSROOM	TESTING

Strengths	Need To Know

Weaknesses	Notes

IEP Meeting Checklist

Student's Name		IEP Due Date	
Date Of Birth		Classification	
Grade		Meeting Date	

♥ Before Meeting ♥

♥ Day of Meeting ♥

♥ After Meeting ♥

⠶⠶ IEP Meeting Notes ⠶⠶

Student's Name		IEP Due Date	
Date Of Birth		Classification	
Grade		Meeting Date	

Attendees ☐ Parent/Guardian   ☐ OT   ☐ PT

☐ Classroom Teacher   ☐ Speech

☐ Other

Meeting Purpose ....

....

....

❦ Parent Concerns ❦

❦ Student's Progress ❦

❦ Next Steps ❦

Progress Monitoring

Progress Monitoring

Student's Name : ....

Grade : ....

Goals			
1		2	
3		4	
5		6	

Goal #	Date	Trial 1	Date	Trial 2	Date	Trial 3

ˇ Comments ˇ

Progress Monitoring

Student's Name : ....   Grade : ....

Goals		
1		2
3		4
5		6

Goal #	Date	Trial 1	Date	Trial 2	Date	Trial 3

⌄ Comments ⌄

Small Group Progress Monitoring

Subject : .... Week of : ....

Date	Target Skill and Activity	Students	Notes

⋙ Communication Log ⋘

MOTHER		FATHER		OTHER CONTACT	
Email		**Email**		**Email**	
Cell		**Cell**		**Cell**	
Work		**Work**		**Work**	

DATE & TIME	TO	METHOD OF CONTACT	REASON FOR CONTACT	FOLLOW UP	NOTES
		☐ Call ☐ Email ☐ Note ☐ Meeting ☐ Other:		☐ YES ☐ NO	
		☐ Call ☐ Email ☐ Note ☐ Meeting ☐ Other:		☐ YES ☐ NO	
		☐ Call ☐ Email ☐ Note ☐ Meeting ☐ Other:		☐ YES ☐ NO	
		☐ Call ☐ Email ☐ Note ☐ Meeting ☐ Other:		☐ YES ☐ NO	
		☐ Call ☐ Email ☐ Note ☐ Meeting ☐ Other:		☐ YES ☐ NO	
		☐ Call ☐ Email ☐ Note ☐ Meeting ☐ Other:		☐ YES ☐ NO	

Communication Log

DATE & TIME	TO	METHOD OF CONTACT	REASON FOR CONTACT	FOLLOW UP	NOTES
		☐ Call ☐ Email ☐ Note ☐ Meeting ☐ Other:		☐ YES ☐ NO	
		☐ Call ☐ Email ☐ Note ☐ Meeting ☐ Other:		☐ YES ☐ NO	
		☐ Call ☐ Email ☐ Note ☐ Meeting ☐ Other:		☐ YES ☐ NO	
		☐ Call ☐ Email ☐ Note ☐ Meeting ☐ Other:		☐ YES ☐ NO	
		☐ Call ☐ Email ☐ Note ☐ Meeting ☐ Other:		☐ YES ☐ NO	
		☐ Call ☐ Email ☐ Note ☐ Meeting ☐ Other:		☐ YES ☐ NO	
		☐ Call ☐ Email ☐ Note ☐ Meeting ☐ Other:		☐ YES ☐ NO	
		☐ Call ☐ Email ☐ Note ☐ Meeting ☐ Other:		☐ YES ☐ NO	

Observations

Date :

Date :

Date :

Date :

Date :

Date :

Date :

Date :

Date :

Observations

Date :

Date :

Date :

Date :

Date :

Date :

Date :

Date :

Date :

▸▸▸ Student's Name ◂◂◂

ID .... Grade ....

Number

Student info

Student's Name		Student ID	
Date Of Birth		Grade	
IEP Expiration Date		ETR Expiration Date	

Contact Info

Name		Name	
Relationship		Relationship	
Phone Number		Phone Number	
Email		Email	

IEP GOALS

Related Services	Time
☐ Occupational Therapy	
☐ Physical Therapy	
☐ Speech Therapy	
☐ Behavioral Therapy	
☐ Other :	

Important Information

Medication	Other

IEP Snapshot

Student's Name: _____ Case Manager: _____ Date of IEP: _____

Disability: _____ Eligibility: _____ Behavior Plan: ☐ **Yes** ☐ **No**

Subject	Goal

Accommodations

IN THE CLASSROOM	TESTING

Strengths	Need To Know

Weaknesses	Notes

IEP Meeting Checklist

Student's Name		IEP Due Date	
Date Of Birth		Classification	
Grade		Meeting Date	

˅ Before Meeting ˅

˅ Day of Meeting ˅

˅ After Meeting ˅

IEP Meeting Notes

Student's Name		IEP Due Date	
Date Of Birth		Classification	
Grade		Meeting Date	

Attendees
- [ ] Parent/Guardian
- [ ] Classroom Teacher
- [ ] Other ....
- [ ] OT
- [ ] Speech
- [ ] PT

Meeting Purpose ....
....
....

❤ Parent Concerns ❤

❤ Student's Progress ❤

❤ Next Steps ❤

▸▸▸ Progress Monitoring

Progress Monitoring

Student's Name : ....   Grade : ....

Goals			
1		2	
3		4	
5		6	

Goal #	Date	Trial 1	Date	Trial 2	Date	Trial 3

⩔ Comments ⩔

Progress Monitoring

Student's Name : ....   Grade : ....

Goals	
1	2
3	4
5	6

Goal #	Date	Trial 1	Date	Trial 2	Date	Trial 3

⌄ Comments ⌄

Small Group Progress
Monitoring

Subject : .... Week of : ....

Date	Target Skill and Activity	Students	Notes

>>> Communication Log <<<

MOTHER	FATHER	OTHER CONTACT
Email	Email	Email
Cell	Cell	Cell
Work	Work	Work

DATE & TIME	TO	METHOD OF CONTACT	REASON FOR CONTACT	FOLLOW UP	NOTES
		☐ Call ☐ Email ☐ Note ☐ Meeting ☐ Other:		☐ YES ☐ NO	
		☐ Call ☐ Email ☐ Note ☐ Meeting ☐ Other:		☐ YES ☐ NO	
		☐ Call ☐ Email ☐ Note ☐ Meeting ☐ Other:		☐ YES ☐ NO	
		☐ Call ☐ Email ☐ Note ☐ Meeting ☐ Other:		☐ YES ☐ NO	
		☐ Call ☐ Email ☐ Note ☐ Meeting ☐ Other:		☐ YES ☐ NO	
		☐ Call ☐ Email ☐ Note ☐ Meeting ☐ Other:		☐ YES ☐ NO	

⠶⠶⠶ Communication Log ⠶⠶⠶

DATE & TIME	TO	METHOD OF CONTACT	REASON FOR CONTACT	FOLLOW UP	NOTES
		☐ Call ☐ Email ☐ Note ☐ Meeting ☐ Other:		☐ YES ☐ NO	
		☐ Call ☐ Email ☐ Note ☐ Meeting ☐ Other:		☐ YES ☐ NO	
		☐ Call ☐ Email ☐ Note ☐ Meeting ☐ Other:		☐ YES ☐ NO	
		☐ Call ☐ Email ☐ Note ☐ Meeting ☐ Other:		☐ YES ☐ NO	
		☐ Call ☐ Email ☐ Note ☐ Meeting ☐ Other:		☐ YES ☐ NO	
		☐ Call ☐ Email ☐ Note ☐ Meeting ☐ Other:		☐ YES ☐ NO	
		☐ Call ☐ Email ☐ Note ☐ Meeting ☐ Other:		☐ YES ☐ NO	
		☐ Call ☐ Email ☐ Note ☐ Meeting ☐ Other:		☐ YES ☐ NO	

Observations

Date :

Date :

Date :

Date :

Date :

Date :

Date :

Date :

Date :

Opservations

Date :

Date :

Date :

Date :

Date :

Date :

Date :

Date :

Date :

▶▶▶ Student's Name ◀◀◀

ID .... Grade ....

Number

Student info

Student's Name		Student ID	
Date Of Birth		Grade	
IEP Expiration Date		ETR Expiration Date	

♥ Contact Info ♥

Name		Name	
Relationship		Relationship	
Phone Number		Phone Number	
Email		Email	

♥ IEP GOALS ♥

♥ Related Services ♥	Time
☐ Occupational Therapy	
☐ Physical Therapy	
☐ Speech Therapy	
☐ Behavioral Therapy	
☐ Other :	

♥ Important Information ♥

Medication	Other

IEP Snapshot

Student's Name: [   ] Case Manager: [   ] Date of IEP: [   ]

Disability: [   ] Eligibility: [   ] Behavior Plan: [ ] **Yes** [ ] **No**

Subject

Goal

Accommodations

IN THE CLASSROOM	TESTING

Strengths

Need To Know

Weaknesses

Notes

IEP Meeting Checklist

Student's Name		IEP Due Date	
Date Of Birth		Classification	
Grade		Meeting Date	

⌄ Before Meeting ⌄

⌄ Day of Meeting ⌄

⌄ After Meeting ⌄

IEP Meeting Notes

Student's Name		IEP Due Date	
Date Of Birth		Classification	
Grade		Meeting Date	

Attendees
☐ Parent/Guardian   ☐ OT   ☐ PT
☐ Classroom Teacher   ☐ Speech
☐ Other

Meeting Purpose ....
....
....

❧ Parent Concerns ❧

❧ Student's Progress ❧

❧ Next Steps ❧

Progress Monitoring

Progress Monitoring

Student's Name : ....   Grade : ....

Goals	
1	2
3	4
5	6

Goal #	Date	Trial 1	Date	Trial 2	Date	Trial 3

⌄ Comments ⌄

Progress Monitoring

Student's Name : ....   Grade : ....

Goals			
1		2	
3		4	
5		6	

Goal #	Date	Trial 1	Date	Trial 2	Date	Trial 3

⌄ Comments ⌄

Small Group Progress
Monitoring

Subject : ....   Week of : ....

Date	Target Skill and Activity	Students	Notes

⋙ Communication Log ⋘

MOTHER	FATHER	OTHER CONTACT
Email	Email	Email
Cell	Cell	Cell
Work	Work	Work

DATE & TIME	TO	METHOD OF CONTACT	REASON FOR CONTACT	FOLLOW UP	NOTES
		☐ Call ☐ Email ☐ Note ☐ Meeting ☐ Other:		☐ YES ☐ NO	
		☐ Call ☐ Email ☐ Note ☐ Meeting ☐ Other:		☐ YES ☐ NO	
		☐ Call ☐ Email ☐ Note ☐ Meeting ☐ Other:		☐ YES ☐ NO	
		☐ Call ☐ Email ☐ Note ☐ Meeting ☐ Other:		☐ YES ☐ NO	
		☐ Call ☐ Email ☐ Note ☐ Meeting ☐ Other:		☐ YES ☐ NO	
		☐ Call ☐ Email ☐ Note ☐ Meeting ☐ Other:		☐ YES ☐ NO	

⠶⠶ Communication Log ⠶⠶

DATE & TIME	TO	METHOD OF CONTACT	REASON FOR CONTACT	FOLLOW UP	NOTES
		☐ Call ☐ Email ☐ Note ☐ Meeting ☐ Other:		☐ YES ☐ NO	
		☐ Call ☐ Email ☐ Note ☐ Meeting ☐ Other:		☐ YES ☐ NO	
		☐ Call ☐ Email ☐ Note ☐ Meeting ☐ Other:		☐ YES ☐ NO	
		☐ Call ☐ Email ☐ Note ☐ Meeting ☐ Other:		☐ YES ☐ NO	
		☐ Call ☐ Email ☐ Note ☐ Meeting ☐ Other:		☐ YES ☐ NO	
		☐ Call ☐ Email ☐ Note ☐ Meeting ☐ Other:		☐ YES ☐ NO	
		☐ Call ☐ Email ☐ Note ☐ Meeting ☐ Other:		☐ YES ☐ NO	
		☐ Call ☐ Email ☐ Note ☐ Meeting ☐ Other:		☐ YES ☐ NO	

Observations

Date :

Date :

Date :

Date :

Date :

Date :

Date :

Date :

Date :

Observations

Date :

Date :

Date :

Date :

Date :

Date :

Date :

Date :

Date :

▶▶▶ Student's Name ◀◀◀

ID .... Grade ....

Number

Student Info

Student's Name		Student ID	
Date Of Birth		Grade	
IEP Expiration Date		ETR Expiration Date	

❤ Contact Info ❤

Name		Name	
Relationship		Relationship	
Phone Number		Phone Number	
Email		Email	

❤ IEP GOALS ❤

❤ Related Services ❤

❤ Related Services ❤	Time
☐ Occupational Therapy	
☐ Physical Therapy	
☐ Speech Therapy	
☐ Behavioral Therapy	
☐ Other :	

❤ Important Information ❤

Medication	Other

IEP Snapshot

Student's Name: [_____]   Case Manager: [_____]   Date of IEP: [_____]

Disability: [_____]   Eligibility: [_____]   Behavior Plan: ☐ **Yes** ☐ **No**

♥ Subject ♥	♥ Goal ♥

♥ Accommodations ♥

IN THE CLASSROOM	TESTING

♥ Strengths ♥	♥ Need To Know ♥

♥ Weaknesses ♥	♥ Notes ♥

IEP Meeting Checklist

Student's Name		IEP Due Date	
Date Of Birth		Classification	
Grade		Meeting Date	

˅ Before Meeting ˅

˅ Day of Meeting ˅

˅ After Meeting ˅

>>> IEP Meeting Notes <<<

Student's Name		**IEP Due Date**	
Date Of Birth		**Classification**	
Grade		**Meeting Date**	

Attendees
- [ ] Parent/Guardian
- [ ] OT
- [ ] PT
- [ ] Classroom Teacher
- [ ] Speech
- [ ] Other ....

Meeting Purpose ....
....
....

❤ Parent Concerns ❤

❤ Student's Progress ❤

❤ Next Steps ❤

⠞⠇⠋ Progress Monitoring

Progress Monitoring

Student's Name : .... Grade : ....

Goals			
1		**2**	
3		**4**	
5		**6**	

Goal #	Date	Trial 1	Date	Trial 2	Date	Trial 3

˅ Comments ˅

Progress Monitoring

Student's Name : ....

Grade : ....

Goals			
1		2	
3		4	
5		6	

Goal #	Date	Trial 1	Date	Trial 2	Date	Trial 3

Comments

Small Group Progress
Monitoring

Subject : ....   Week of : ....

Date	Target Skill and Activity	Students	Notes

⠶⠶⠶ Communication Log ⠶⠶⠶

MOTHER		FATHER		OTHER CONTACT	
Email		Email		Email	
Cell		Cell		Cell	
Work		Work		Work	

DATE & TIME	TO	METHOD OF CONTACT	REASON FOR CONTACT	FOLLOW UP	NOTES
		☐ Call ☐ Email ☐ Note ☐ Meeting ☐ Other:		☐ YES ☐ NO	
		☐ Call ☐ Email ☐ Note ☐ Meeting ☐ Other:		☐ YES ☐ NO	
		☐ Call ☐ Email ☐ Note ☐ Meeting ☐ Other:		☐ YES ☐ NO	
		☐ Call ☐ Email ☐ Note ☐ Meeting ☐ Other:		☐ YES ☐ NO	
		☐ Call ☐ Email ☐ Note ☐ Meeting ☐ Other:		☐ YES ☐ NO	
		☐ Call ☐ Email ☐ Note ☐ Meeting ☐ Other:		☐ YES ☐ NO	

Communication Log

DATE & TIME	TO	METHOD OF CONTACT	REASON FOR CONTACT	FOLLOW UP	NOTES
		☐ Call ☐ Email ☐ Note ☐ Meeting ☐ Other:		☐ YES ☐ NO	
		☐ Call ☐ Email ☐ Note ☐ Meeting ☐ Other:		☐ YES ☐ NO	
		☐ Call ☐ Email ☐ Note ☐ Meeting ☐ Other:		☐ YES ☐ NO	
		☐ Call ☐ Email ☐ Note ☐ Meeting ☐ Other:		☐ YES ☐ NO	
		☐ Call ☐ Email ☐ Note ☐ Meeting ☐ Other:		☐ YES ☐ NO	
		☐ Call ☐ Email ☐ Note ☐ Meeting ☐ Other:		☐ YES ☐ NO	
		☐ Call ☐ Email ☐ Note ☐ Meeting ☐ Other:		☐ YES ☐ NO	
		☐ Call ☐ Email ☐ Note ☐ Meeting ☐ Other:		☐ YES ☐ NO	

Observations

Date :

Date :

Date :

Date :

Date :

Date :

Date :

Date :

Date :

Observations

Date :

Date :

Date :

Date :

Date :

Date :

Date :

Date :

Date :

▶▶▶ Student's Name ◀◀◀

ID ....   Grade ....

Number

Student info

Student's Name		Student ID	
Date Of Birth		Grade	
IEP Expiration Date		ETR Expiration Date	

❣ Contact Info ❣

Name		Name	
Relationship		Relationship	
Phone Number		Phone Number	
Email		Email	

❣ IEP GOALS ❣

❣ Related Services ❣	Time
☐ Occupational Therapy	
☐ Physical Therapy	
☐ Speech Therapy	
☐ Behavioral Therapy	
☐ Other :	

❣ Important Information ❣

Medication	Other

IEP Snapshot

Student's Name: [   ] Case Manager: [   ] Date of IEP: [   ]

Disability: [   ] Eligibility: [   ] Behavior Plan: [ ] **Yes** [ ] **No**

Subject / Goal

Accommodations

IN THE CLASSROOM	TESTING

Strengths

Need To Know

Weaknesses

Notes

IEP Meeting Checklist

Student's Name		IEP Due Date	
Date Of Birth		Classification	
Grade		Meeting Date	

Before Meeting

Day of Meeting

After Meeting

IEP Meeting Notes

Student's Name		IEP Due Date	
Date Of Birth		Classification	
Grade		Meeting Date	

Attendees
☐ Parent/Guardian   ☐ OT   ☐ PT
☐ Classroom Teacher   ☐ Speech
☐ Other

Meeting Purpose
....
....
....

♥ Parent Concerns ♥

♥ Student's Progress ♥

♥ Next Steps ♥

Progress Monitoring

Progress Monitoring

Student's Name : .... Grade : ....

Goals	
1	2 ....
3	4 ....
5	6 ....

Goal #	Date	Trial 1	Date	Trial 2	Date	Trial 3

⌄ Comments ⌄

Progress Monitoring

Student's Name : .... Grade : ....

Goals			
1		2	
3		4	
5		6	

Goal #	Date	Trial 1	Date	Trial 2	Date	Trial 3

❯ Comments ❮

Small Group Progress
Monitoring

Subject : .... Week of : ....

Date	Target Skill and Activity	Students	Notes

Communication Log

MOTHER	FATHER	OTHER CONTACT
Email	Email	Email
Cell	Cell	Cell
Work	Work	Work

DATE & TIME	TO	METHOD OF CONTACT	REASON FOR CONTACT	FOLLOW UP	NOTES
		☐ Call ☐ Email ☐ Note ☐ Meeting ☐ Other:		☐ YES ☐ NO	
		☐ Call ☐ Email ☐ Note ☐ Meeting ☐ Other:		☐ YES ☐ NO	
		☐ Call ☐ Email ☐ Note ☐ Meeting ☐ Other:		☐ YES ☐ NO	
		☐ Call ☐ Email ☐ Note ☐ Meeting ☐ Other:		☐ YES ☐ NO	
		☐ Call ☐ Email ☐ Note ☐ Meeting ☐ Other:		☐ YES ☐ NO	
		☐ Call ☐ Email ☐ Note ☐ Meeting ☐ Other:		☐ YES ☐ NO	

>>> Communication Log <<<

DATE & TIME	TO	METHOD OF CONTACT	REASON FOR CONTACT	FOLLOW UP	NOTES
		☐ Call ☐ Email ☐ Note ☐ Meeting ☐ Other:		☐ YES ☐ NO	
		☐ Call ☐ Email ☐ Note ☐ Meeting ☐ Other:		☐ YES ☐ NO	
		☐ Call ☐ Email ☐ Note ☐ Meeting ☐ Other:		☐ YES ☐ NO	
		☐ Call ☐ Email ☐ Note ☐ Meeting ☐ Other:		☐ YES ☐ NO	
		☐ Call ☐ Email ☐ Note ☐ Meeting ☐ Other:		☐ YES ☐ NO	
		☐ Call ☐ Email ☐ Note ☐ Meeting ☐ Other:		☐ YES ☐ NO	
		☐ Call ☐ Email ☐ Note ☐ Meeting ☐ Other:		☐ YES ☐ NO	
		☐ Call ☐ Email ☐ Note ☐ Meeting ☐ Other:		☐ YES ☐ NO	

Observations

Date :

Date :

Date :

Date :

Date :

Date :

Date :

Date :

Date :

Observations

Date :

Date :

Date :

Date :

Date :

Date :

Date :

Date :

Date :

▶▶▶ Student's Name ◀◀◀

┌─────────────────────────────┐
│   │
│   │
│   │
└─────────────────────────────┘

ID .... Grade ....

Number

┌─────────┐
│   │
│   │
└─────────┘

Student info

Student's Name		Student ID	
Date Of Birth		Grade	
IEP Expiration Date		ETR Expiration Date	

ᵛ Contact Info ᵛ

Name		Name	
Relationship		Relationship	
Phone Number		Phone Number	
Email		Email	

ᵛ IEP GOALS ᵛ

ᵛ Related Services ᵛ	Time
☐ Occupational Therapy	
☐ Physical Therapy	
☐ Speech Therapy	
☐ Behavioral Therapy	
☐ Other :	

ᵛ Important Information ᵛ

Medication	Other

IEP Snapshot

Student's Name: _____ Case Manager: _____ Date of IEP: _____

Disability: _____ Eligibility: _____ Behavior Plan: ☐ **Yes** ☐ **No**

❥ Subject ❥	❥ Goal ❥

❥ Accommodations ❥

IN THE CLASSROOM	TESTING

❥ Strengths ❥	❥ Need To Know ❥

❥ Weaknesses ❥	❥ Notes ❥

IEP Meeting Checklist

Student's Name		IEP Due Date	
Date Of Birth		Classification	
Grade		Meeting Date	

Before Meeting

Day of Meeting

After Meeting

IEP Meeting Notes

Student's Name		IEP Due Date	
Date Of Birth		Classification	
Grade		Meeting Date	

Attendees
- ☐ Parent/Guardian
- ☐ Classroom Teacher
- ☐ Other
- ☐ OT
- ☐ Speech
- ☐ PT

Meeting Purpose ....
....
....

❥ Parent Concerns ❥

❥ Student's Progress ❥

❥ Next Steps ❥

Progress Monitoring

Progress Monitoring

Student's Name : .... Grade : ....

Goals			
1		2	
3		4	
5		6	

Goal #	Date	Trial 1	Date	Trial 2	Date	Trial 3

Comments

Progress Monitoring

Student's Name : .... Grade : ....

Goals			
1		2	
3		4	
5		6	

Goal #	Date	Trial 1	Date	Trial 2	Date	Trial 3

⌄ Comments ⌄

Small Group Progress
Monitoring

Subject : ....   Week of : ....

Date	Target Skill and Activity	Students	Notes

>>> Communication Log <<<

MOTHER		FATHER		OTHER CONTACT	
Email		Email		Email	
Cell		Cell		Cell	
Work		Work		Work	

DATE & TIME	TO	METHOD OF CONTACT	REASON FOR CONTACT	FOLLOW UP	NOTES
		☐ Call ☐ Email ☐ Note ☐ Meeting ☐ Other:		☐ YES ☐ NO	
		☐ Call ☐ Email ☐ Note ☐ Meeting ☐ Other:		☐ YES ☐ NO	
		☐ Call ☐ Email ☐ Note ☐ Meeting ☐ Other:		☐ YES ☐ NO	
		☐ Call ☐ Email ☐ Note ☐ Meeting ☐ Other:		☐ YES ☐ NO	
		☐ Call ☐ Email ☐ Note ☐ Meeting ☐ Other:		☐ YES ☐ NO	
		☐ Call ☐ Email ☐ Note ☐ Meeting ☐ Other:		☐ YES ☐ NO	

Communication Log

DATE & TIME	TO	METHOD OF CONTACT	REASON FOR CONTACT	FOLLOW UP	NOTES
		☐ Call ☐ Email ☐ Note ☐ Meeting ☐ Other:		☐ YES ☐ NO	
		☐ Call ☐ Email ☐ Note ☐ Meeting ☐ Other:		☐ YES ☐ NO	
		☐ Call ☐ Email ☐ Note ☐ Meeting ☐ Other:		☐ YES ☐ NO	
		☐ Call ☐ Email ☐ Note ☐ Meeting ☐ Other:		☐ YES ☐ NO	
		☐ Call ☐ Email ☐ Note ☐ Meeting ☐ Other:		☐ YES ☐ NO	
		☐ Call ☐ Email ☐ Note ☐ Meeting ☐ Other:		☐ YES ☐ NO	
		☐ Call ☐ Email ☐ Note ☐ Meeting ☐ Other:		☐ YES ☐ NO	
		☐ Call ☐ Email ☐ Note ☐ Meeting ☐ Other:		☐ YES ☐ NO	

Observations

Date :

Date :

Date :

Date :

Date :

Date :

Date :

Date :

Date :

Observations

Date :

Date :

Date :

Date :

Date :

Date :

Date :

Date :

Date :

▶▶▶ Student's Name ◀◀◀

ID .... Grade ....

Number

Student info

Student's Name		Student ID	
Date Of Birth		Grade	
IEP Expiration Date		ETR Expiration Date	

❣ Contact Info ❣

Name		Name	
Relationship		Relationship	
Phone Number		Phone Number	
Email		Email	

❣ IEP GOALS ❣

❣ Related Services ❣	Time
☐ Occupational Therapy	
☐ Physical Therapy	
☐ Speech Therapy	
☐ Behavioral Therapy	
☐ Other :	

❣ Important Information ❣

Medication	Other

IEP Snapshot

Student's Name: _____ Case Manager: _____ Date of IEP: _____

Disability: _____ Eligibility: _____ Behavior Plan: ☐ **Yes** ☐ **No**

♥ Subject ♥	♥ Goal ♥

♥ Accommodations ♥

IN THE CLASSROOM	TESTING

♥ Strengths ♥	♥ Need To Know ♥

♥ Weaknesses ♥	♥ Notes ♥

IEP Meeting Checklist

Student's Name		IEP Due Date	
Date Of Birth		Classification	
Grade		Meeting Date	

Before Meeting

Day of Meeting

After Meeting

IEP Meeting Notes

Student's Name		IEP Due Date	
Date Of Birth		Classification	
Grade		Meeting Date	

Attendees ☐ Parent/Guardian ☐ OT ☐ PT

☐ Classroom Teacher ☐ Speech

☐ Other

Meeting Purpose

♥ Parent Concerns ♥

♥ Student's Progress ♥

♥ Next Steps ♥

Progress Monitoring

Progress Monitoring

Student's Name : .... Grade : ....

Goals	
1	2
3	4
5	6

Goal #	Date	Trial 1	Date	Trial 2	Date	Trial 3

Comments

Progress Monitoring

Student's Name : .... Grade : ....

Goals			
1		2	
3		4	
5		6	

Goal #	Date	Trial 1	Date	Trial 2	Date	Trial 3

∨ Comments ∨

Small Group Progress
Monitoring

Subject : ....   Week of : ....

Date	Target Skill and Activity	Students	Notes

>>> Communication Log <<<

MOTHER	FATHER	OTHER CONTACT
Email	**Email**	**Email**
Cell	**Cell**	**Cell**
Work	**Work**	**Work**

DATE & TIME	TO	METHOD OF CONTACT	REASON FOR CONTACT	FOLLOW UP	NOTES
		☐ Call ☐ Email ☐ Note ☐ Meeting ☐ Other:		☐ YES ☐ NO	
		☐ Call ☐ Email ☐ Note ☐ Meeting ☐ Other:		☐ YES ☐ NO	
		☐ Call ☐ Email ☐ Note ☐ Meeting ☐ Other:		☐ YES ☐ NO	
		☐ Call ☐ Email ☐ Note ☐ Meeting ☐ Other:		☐ YES ☐ NO	
		☐ Call ☐ Email ☐ Note ☐ Meeting ☐ Other:		☐ YES ☐ NO	
		☐ Call ☐ Email ☐ Note ☐ Meeting ☐ Other:		☐ YES ☐ NO	

Communication Log

DATE & TIME	TO	METHOD OF CONTACT	REASON FOR CONTACT	FOLLOW UP	NOTES
		☐ Call ☐ Email ☐ Note ☐ Meeting ☐ Other:		☐ YES ☐ NO	
		☐ Call ☐ Email ☐ Note ☐ Meeting ☐ Other:		☐ YES ☐ NO	
		☐ Call ☐ Email ☐ Note ☐ Meeting ☐ Other:		☐ YES ☐ NO	
		☐ Call ☐ Email ☐ Note ☐ Meeting ☐ Other:		☐ YES ☐ NO	
		☐ Call ☐ Email ☐ Note ☐ Meeting ☐ Other:		☐ YES ☐ NO	
		☐ Call ☐ Email ☐ Note ☐ Meeting ☐ Other:		☐ YES ☐ NO	
		☐ Call ☐ Email ☐ Note ☐ Meeting ☐ Other:		☐ YES ☐ NO	
		☐ Call ☐ Email ☐ Note ☐ Meeting ☐ Other:		☐ YES ☐ NO	

Observations

Date :

Date :

Date :

Date :

Date :

Date :

Date :

Date :

Date :

Opservations

Date :

Date :

Date :

Date :

Date :

Date :

Date :

Date :

Date :

▶▶▶ Student's Name ◀◀◀

ID .... Grade ....

Number

Student info

Student's Name		Student ID	
Date Of Birth		Grade	
IEP Expiration Date		ETR Expiration Date	

❤ Contact Info ❤

Name		Name	
Relationship		Relationship	
Phone Number		Phone Number	
Email		Email	

❤ IEP GOALS ❤

❤ Related Services ❤ — Time

	Related Services	Time
☐	Occupational Therapy	
☐	Physical Therapy	
☐	Speech Therapy	
☐	Behavioral Therapy	
☐	Other :	

❤ Important Information ❤

Medication	Other

IEP Snapshot

Student's Name: [   ]   Case Manager: [   ]   Date of IEP: [   ]

Disability: [   ]   Eligibility: [   ]   Behavior Plan: [ ] Yes [ ] No

Subject	Goal

Accommodations

IN THE CLASSROOM	TESTING

Strengths	Need To Know

Weaknesses	Notes

IEP Meeting Checklist

Student's Name		IEP Due Date	
Date Of Birth		Classification	
Grade		Meeting Date	

❤ Before Meeting ❤

❤ Day of Meeting ❤

❤ After Meeting ❤

IEP Meeting Notes

Student's Name		IEP Due Date	
Date Of Birth		Classification	
Grade		Meeting Date	

Attendees
- ☐ Parent/Guardian
- ☐ Classroom Teacher
- ☐ Other ....
- ☐ OT
- ☐ Speech
- ☐ PT

Meeting Purpose
....
....
....

❥ Parent Concerns ❥

❥ Student's Progress ❥

❥ Next Steps ❥

Progress Monitoring

Progress Monitoring

Student's Name : ....   Grade : ....

Goals			
1		2	
3		4	
5		6	

Goal #	Date	Trial 1	Date	Trial 2	Date	Trial 3

❤ Comments ❤

Progress Monitoring

Student's Name : .... Grade : ....

Goals			
1		**2**	
3		**4**	
5		**6**	

Goal #	Date	Trial 1	Date	Trial 2	Date	Trial 3

⌄ Comments ⌄

Small Group Progress
Monitoring

Subject : ....   Week of : ....

Date	Target Skill and Activity	Students	Notes

>>> Communication Log <<<

MOTHER		FATHER		OTHER CONTACT	
Email		Email		Email	
Cell		Cell		Cell	
Work		Work		Work	

DATE & TIME	TO	METHOD OF CONTACT	REASON FOR CONTACT	FOLLOW UP	NOTES
		☐ Call ☐ Email ☐ Note ☐ Meeting ☐ Other:		☐ YES ☐ NO	
		☐ Call ☐ Email ☐ Note ☐ Meeting ☐ Other:		☐ YES ☐ NO	
		☐ Call ☐ Email ☐ Note ☐ Meeting ☐ Other:		☐ YES ☐ NO	
		☐ Call ☐ Email ☐ Note ☐ Meeting ☐ Other:		☐ YES ☐ NO	
		☐ Call ☐ Email ☐ Note ☐ Meeting ☐ Other:		☐ YES ☐ NO	
		☐ Call ☐ Email ☐ Note ☐ Meeting ☐ Other:		☐ YES ☐ NO	

⋙ Communication Log ⋘

DATE & TIME	TO	METHOD OF CONTACT	REASON FOR CONTACT	FOLLOW UP	NOTES
		☐ Call ☐ Email ☐ Note ☐ Meeting ☐ Other:		☐ YES ☐ NO	
		☐ Call ☐ Email ☐ Note ☐ Meeting ☐ Other:		☐ YES ☐ NO	
		☐ Call ☐ Email ☐ Note ☐ Meeting ☐ Other:		☐ YES ☐ NO	
		☐ Call ☐ Email ☐ Note ☐ Meeting ☐ Other:		☐ YES ☐ NO	
		☐ Call ☐ Email ☐ Note ☐ Meeting ☐ Other:		☐ YES ☐ NO	
		☐ Call ☐ Email ☐ Note ☐ Meeting ☐ Other:		☐ YES ☐ NO	
		☐ Call ☐ Email ☐ Note ☐ Meeting ☐ Other:		☐ YES ☐ NO	
		☐ Call ☐ Email ☐ Note ☐ Meeting ☐ Other:		☐ YES ☐ NO	

Observations

Date :

Date :

Date :

Date :

Date :

Date :

Date :

Date :

Date :

Observations

Date :

Date :

Date :

Date :

Date :

Date :

Date :

Date :

Date :

▶▶▶ Student's Name ◀◀◀

ID .... Grade ....

Number

Student info

Student's Name		Student ID	
Date Of Birth		Grade	
IEP Expiration Date		ETR Expiration Date	

⋎ Contact Info ⋎

Name		Name	
Relationship		Relationship	
Phone Number		Phone Number	
Email		Email	

⋎ IEP GOALS ⋎

⋎ Related Services ⋎	Time
☐ Occupational Therapy	
☐ Physical Therapy	
☐ Speech Therapy	
☐ Behavioral Therapy	
☐ Other :	

⋎ Important Information ⋎	
Medication	Other

IEP Snapshot

Student's Name: _____   Case Manager: _____   Date of IEP: _____

Disability: _____   Eligibility: _____   Behavior Plan: ☐ **Yes** ☐ **No**

ꕥ Subject ꕥ	ꕥ Goal ꕥ

ꕥ Accommodations ꕥ

IN THE CLASSROOM	TESTING

ꕥ Strengths ꕥ	ꕥ Need To Know ꕥ

ꕥ Weaknesses ꕥ	ꕥ Notes ꕥ

IEP Meeting Checklist

Student's Name		IEP Due Date	
Date Of Birth		Classification	
Grade		Meeting Date	

❤ Before Meeting ❤

❤ Day of Meeting ❤

❤ After Meeting ❤

>>> IEP Meeting Notes <<<

Student's Name		**IEP Due Date**	
Date Of Birth		**Classification**	
Grade		**Meeting Date**	

Attendees ☐ Parent/Guardian ☐ OT ☐ PT

☐ Classroom Teacher ☐ Speech

☐ Other ....

Meeting Purpose ....
....
....

♥ Parent Concerns ♥

♥ Student's Progress ♥

♥ Next Steps ♥

Progress Monitoring

Progress Monitoring

Student's Name : .... Grade : ....

Goals			
1		2	
3		4	
5		6	

Goal #	Date	Trial 1	Date	Trial 2	Date	Trial 3

⌄ Comments ⌄

⋙ Progress Monitoring ⋘

Student's Name : ....   Grade : ....

Goals			
1		2	
3		4	
5		6	

Goal #	Date	Trial 1	Date	Trial 2	Date	Trial 3

⌄ Comments ⌄

Small Group Progress
Monitoring

Subject : ....   Week of : ....

Date	Target Skill and Activity	Students	Notes

⠶⠶⠶ Communication Log ⠶⠶⠶

MOTHER		FATHER		OTHER CONTACT	
Email		Email		Email	
Cell		Cell		Cell	
Work		Work		Work	

DATE & TIME	TO	METHOD OF CONTACT	REASON FOR CONTACT	FOLLOW UP	NOTES
		☐ Call ☐ Email ☐ Note ☐ Meeting ☐ Other:		☐ YES ☐ NO	
		☐ Call ☐ Email ☐ Note ☐ Meeting ☐ Other:		☐ YES ☐ NO	
		☐ Call ☐ Email ☐ Note ☐ Meeting ☐ Other:		☐ YES ☐ NO	
		☐ Call ☐ Email ☐ Note ☐ Meeting ☐ Other:		☐ YES ☐ NO	
		☐ Call ☐ Email ☐ Note ☐ Meeting ☐ Other:		☐ YES ☐ NO	
		☐ Call ☐ Email ☐ Note ☐ Meeting ☐ Other:		☐ YES ☐ NO	

Communication Log

DATE & TIME	TO	METHOD OF CONTACT	REASON FOR CONTACT	FOLLOW UP	NOTES
		☐ Call ☐ Email ☐ Note ☐ Meeting ☐ Other:		☐ YES ☐ NO	
		☐ Call ☐ Email ☐ Note ☐ Meeting ☐ Other:		☐ YES ☐ NO	
		☐ Call ☐ Email ☐ Note ☐ Meeting ☐ Other:		☐ YES ☐ NO	
		☐ Call ☐ Email ☐ Note ☐ Meeting ☐ Other:		☐ YES ☐ NO	
		☐ Call ☐ Email ☐ Note ☐ Meeting ☐ Other:		☐ YES ☐ NO	
		☐ Call ☐ Email ☐ Note ☐ Meeting ☐ Other:		☐ YES ☐ NO	
		☐ Call ☐ Email ☐ Note ☐ Meeting ☐ Other:		☐ YES ☐ NO	
		☐ Call ☐ Email ☐ Note ☐ Meeting ☐ Other:		☐ YES ☐ NO	

Observations

Date : ....

Date : ....

Date : ....

Date : ....

Date : ....

Date : ....

Date : ....

Date : ....

Date : ....

Observations

Date :

Date :

Date :

Date :

Date :

Date :

Date :

Date :

Date :

▶▶▶ Student's Name ◀◀◀

ID .... Grade ....

Number

Student info

Student's Name		Student ID	
Date Of Birth		Grade	
IEP Expiration Date		ETR Expiration Date	

⋎ Contact Info ⋎

Name		Name	
Relationship		Relationship	
Phone Number		Phone Number	
Email		Email	

⋎ IEP GOALS ⋎

⋎ Related Services ⋎

	Time
☐ Occupational Therapy	
☐ Physical Therapy	
☐ Speech Therapy	
☐ Behavioral Therapy	
☐ Other :	

⋎ Important Information ⋎

Medication	Other

IEP Snapshot

Student's Name: [ ] Case Manager: [ ] Date of IEP: [ ]

Disability: [ ] Eligibility: [ ] Behavior Plan: [ ] **Yes** [ ] **No**

⅍ Subject ⅍	⅍ Goal ⅍

⅍ Accommodations ⅍

IN THE CLASSROOM	TESTING

⅍ Strengths ⅍	⅍ Need To Know ⅍

⅍ Weaknesses ⅍	⅍ Notes ⅍

IEP Meeting Checklist

Student's Name		IEP Due Date	
Date Of Birth		Classification	
Grade		Meeting Date	

Before Meeting

Day of Meeting

After Meeting

IEP Meeting Notes

Student's Name		IEP Due Date	
Date Of Birth		Classification	
Grade		Meeting Date	

Attendees ☐ Parent/Guardian ☐ OT ☐ PT

☐ Classroom Teacher ☐ Speech

☐ Other

Meeting Purpose

♥ Parent Concerns ♥

♥ Student's Progress ♥

♥ Next Steps ♥

Progress Monitoring

⠿ Progress Monitoring ⠿

Student's Name : ....   Grade : ....

Goals			
1		**2**	
3		**4**	
5		**6**	

Goal #	Date	Trial 1	Date	Trial 2	Date	Trial 3

⋎ Comments ⋎

Progress Monitoring

Student's Name : ....   Grade : ....

	Goals		
1		2	
3		4	
5		6	

Goal #	Date	Trial 1	Date	Trial 2	Date	Trial 3

❦ Comments ❦

Small Group Progress
Monitoring

Subject : .... Week of : ....

Date	Target Skill and Activity	Students	Notes

>>> Communication Log <<<

MOTHER		FATHER		OTHER CONTACT	
Email		Email		Email	
Cell		Cell		Cell	
Work		Work		Work	

DATE & TIME	TO	METHOD OF CONTACT	REASON FOR CONTACT	FOLLOW UP	NOTES
		☐ Call ☐ Email ☐ Note ☐ Meeting ☐ Other:		☐ YES ☐ NO	
		☐ Call ☐ Email ☐ Note ☐ Meeting ☐ Other:		☐ YES ☐ NO	
		☐ Call ☐ Email ☐ Note ☐ Meeting ☐ Other:		☐ YES ☐ NO	
		☐ Call ☐ Email ☐ Note ☐ Meeting ☐ Other:		☐ YES ☐ NO	
		☐ Call ☐ Email ☐ Note ☐ Meeting ☐ Other:		☐ YES ☐ NO	
		☐ Call ☐ Email ☐ Note ☐ Meeting ☐ Other:		☐ YES ☐ NO	

⠶⠶ Communication Log ⠶⠶

DATE & TIME	TO	METHOD OF CONTACT	REASON FOR CONTACT	FOLLOW UP	NOTES
		☐ Call ☐ Email ☐ Note ☐ Meeting ☐ Other:		☐ YES ☐ NO	
		☐ Call ☐ Email ☐ Note ☐ Meeting ☐ Other:		☐ YES ☐ NO	
		☐ Call ☐ Email ☐ Note ☐ Meeting ☐ Other:		☐ YES ☐ NO	
		☐ Call ☐ Email ☐ Note ☐ Meeting ☐ Other:		☐ YES ☐ NO	
		☐ Call ☐ Email ☐ Note ☐ Meeting ☐ Other:		☐ YES ☐ NO	
		☐ Call ☐ Email ☐ Note ☐ Meeting ☐ Other:		☐ YES ☐ NO	
		☐ Call ☐ Email ☐ Note ☐ Meeting ☐ Other:		☐ YES ☐ NO	
		☐ Call ☐ Email ☐ Note ☐ Meeting ☐ Other:		☐ YES ☐ NO	

Observations

Date :

Date :

Date :

Date :

Date :

Date :

Date :

Date :

Date :

Observations

Date :

Date :

Date :

Date :

Date :

Date :

Date :

Date :

Date :

▶▶▶ Student's Name ◀◀◀

ID .... Grade ....

Number

Student info

Student's Name		Student ID	
Date Of Birth		Grade	
IEP Expiration Date		ETR Expiration Date	

Contact Info

Name		Name	
Relationship		Relationship	
Phone Number		Phone Number	
Email		Email	

IEP GOALS

Related Services	Time
☐ Occupational Therapy	
☐ Physical Therapy	
☐ Speech Therapy	
☐ Behavioral Therapy	
☐ Other :	

Important Information	
Medication	Other

IEP Snapshot

Student's Name: _____ Case Manager: _____ Date of IEP: _____

Disability: _____ Eligibility: _____ Behavior Plan: ☐ **Yes** ☐ **No**

♥ Subject ♥	♥ Goal ♥

♥ Accommodations ♥

IN THE CLASSROOM	TESTING

♥ Strengths ♥	♥ Need To Know ♥

♥ Weaknesses ♥	♥ Notes ♥

>>> IEP Meeting Checklist <<<

Student's Name		IEP Due Date	
Date Of Birth		Classification	
Grade		Meeting Date	

⌄ Before Meeting ⌄

⌄ Day of Meeting ⌄

⌄ After Meeting ⌄

>>> IEP Meeting Notes <<<

Student's Name		**IEP Due Date**	
Date Of Birth		**Classification**	
Grade		**Meeting Date**	

Attendees

☐ Parent/Guardian   ☐ OT   ☐ PT

☐ Classroom Teacher   ☐ Speech

☐ Other _____

Meeting Purpose

....
....
....

❤ Parent Concerns ❤

❤ Student's Progress ❤

❤ Next Steps ❤

>>> 221

⏩ Progress Monitoring

Progress Monitoring

Student's Name : .... Grade : ....

Goals			
1		2	
3		4	
5		6	

Goal #	Date	Trial 1	Date	Trial 2	Date	Trial 3

❤ Comments ❤

Progress Monitoring

Student's Name : ....   Grade : ....

Goals	
1	**2**
3	**4**
5	**6**

Goal #	Date	Trial 1	Date	Trial 2	Date	Trial 3

❤ Comments ❤

Small Group Progress
Monitoring

Subject : ....   Week of : ....

Date	Target Skill and Activity	Students	Notes

>>> Communication Log <<<

MOTHER		FATHER		OTHER CONTACT	
Email		Email		Email	
Cell		Cell		Cell	
Work		Work		Work	

DATE & TIME	TO	METHOD OF CONTACT	REASON FOR CONTACT	FOLLOW UP	NOTES
		☐ Call ☐ Email ☐ Note ☐ Meeting ☐ Other:		☐ YES ☐ NO	
		☐ Call ☐ Email ☐ Note ☐ Meeting ☐ Other:		☐ YES ☐ NO	
		☐ Call ☐ Email ☐ Note ☐ Meeting ☐ Other:		☐ YES ☐ NO	
		☐ Call ☐ Email ☐ Note ☐ Meeting ☐ Other:		☐ YES ☐ NO	
		☐ Call ☐ Email ☐ Note ☐ Meeting ☐ Other:		☐ YES ☐ NO	
		☐ Call ☐ Email ☐ Note ☐ Meeting ☐ Other:		☐ YES ☐ NO	

>>> Communication Log <<<

DATE & TIME	TO	METHOD OF CONTACT	REASON FOR CONTACT	FOLLOW UP	NOTES
		☐ Call ☐ Email ☐ Note ☐ Meeting ☐ Other:		☐ YES ☐ NO	
		☐ Call ☐ Email ☐ Note ☐ Meeting ☐ Other:		☐ YES ☐ NO	
		☐ Call ☐ Email ☐ Note ☐ Meeting ☐ Other:		☐ YES ☐ NO	
		☐ Call ☐ Email ☐ Note ☐ Meeting ☐ Other:		☐ YES ☐ NO	
		☐ Call ☐ Email ☐ Note ☐ Meeting ☐ Other:		☐ YES ☐ NO	
		☐ Call ☐ Email ☐ Note ☐ Meeting ☐ Other:		☐ YES ☐ NO	
		☐ Call ☐ Email ☐ Note ☐ Meeting ☐ Other:		☐ YES ☐ NO	
		☐ Call ☐ Email ☐ Note ☐ Meeting ☐ Other:		☐ YES ☐ NO	

Observations

Date :

Date :

Date :

Date :

Date :

Date :

Date :

Date :

Date :

Observations

Date :

Date :

Date :

Date :

Date :

Date :

Date :

Date :

Date :

▶▶▶ Student's Name ◀◀◀

ID .... Grade ....

Number

Student info

Student's Name		Student ID	
Date Of Birth		Grade	
IEP Expiration Date		ETR Expiration Date	

ⅴ Contact Info ⅴ

Name		Name	
Relationship		Relationship	
Phone Number		Phone Number	
Email		Email	

ⅴ IEP GOALS ⅴ

ⅴ Related Services ⅴ	Time
☐ Occupational Therapy	
☐ Physical Therapy	
☐ Speech Therapy	
☐ Behavioral Therapy	
☐ Other :	

ⅴ Important Information ⅴ	
Medication	Other

IEP Snapshot

Student's Name: _____ Case Manager: _____ Date of IEP: _____

Disability: _____ Eligibility: _____ Behavior Plan: ☐ **Yes** ☐ **No**

❤ Subject ❤	❤ Goal ❤

❤ Accommodations ❤

IN THE CLASSROOM	TESTING

❤ Strengths ❤	❤ Need To Know ❤

❤ Weaknesses ❤	❤ Notes ❤

IEP Meeting Checklist

Student's Name		IEP Due Date	
Date Of Birth		Classification	
Grade		Meeting Date	

⌄ Before Meeting ⌄

⌄ Day of Meeting ⌄

⌄ After Meeting ⌄

IEP Meeting Notes

Student's Name		IEP Due Date	
Date Of Birth		Classification	
Grade		Meeting Date	

Attendees
☐ Parent/Guardian ☐ OT ☐ PT
☐ Classroom Teacher ☐ Speech
☐ Other

Meeting Purpose
....
....
....

♥ Parent Concerns ♥

♥ Student's Progress ♥

♥ Next Steps ♥

Progress Monitoring

>>> Progress Monitoring <<<

Student's Name : .... Grade : ....

Goals			
1		2	
3		4	
5		6	

Goal #	Date	Trial 1	Date	Trial 2	Date	Trial 3

☙ Comments ☙

>>> Progress Monitoring <<<

Student's Name : ....   Grade : ....

Goals			
1		**2**	
3		**4**	
5		**6**	

Goal #	Date	Trial 1	Date	Trial 2	Date	Trial 3

⌄ Comments ⌄

Small Group Progress
Monitoring

Subject : ....   Week of : ....

Date	Target Skill and Activity	Students	Notes

>>> Communication Log <<<

MOTHER	FATHER	OTHER CONTACT
Email	Email	Email
Cell	Cell	Cell
Work	Work	Work

DATE & TIME	TO	METHOD OF CONTACT	REASON FOR CONTACT	FOLLOW UP	NOTES
		☐ Call ☐ Email ☐ Note ☐ Meeting ☐ Other:		☐ YES ☐ NO	
		☐ Call ☐ Email ☐ Note ☐ Meeting ☐ Other:		☐ YES ☐ NO	
		☐ Call ☐ Email ☐ Note ☐ Meeting ☐ Other:		☐ YES ☐ NO	
		☐ Call ☐ Email ☐ Note ☐ Meeting ☐ Other:		☐ YES ☐ NO	
		☐ Call ☐ Email ☐ Note ☐ Meeting ☐ Other:		☐ YES ☐ NO	
		☐ Call ☐ Email ☐ Note ☐ Meeting ☐ Other:		☐ YES ☐ NO	

>>> Communication Log <<<

DATE & TIME	TO	METHOD OF CONTACT	REASON FOR CONTACT	FOLLOW UP	NOTES
		☐ Call ☐ Email ☐ Note ☐ Meeting ☐ Other:		☐ YES ☐ NO	
		☐ Call ☐ Email ☐ Note ☐ Meeting ☐ Other:		☐ YES ☐ NO	
		☐ Call ☐ Email ☐ Note ☐ Meeting ☐ Other:		☐ YES ☐ NO	
		☐ Call ☐ Email ☐ Note ☐ Meeting ☐ Other:		☐ YES ☐ NO	
		☐ Call ☐ Email ☐ Note ☐ Meeting ☐ Other:		☐ YES ☐ NO	
		☐ Call ☐ Email ☐ Note ☐ Meeting ☐ Other:		☐ YES ☐ NO	
		☐ Call ☐ Email ☐ Note ☐ Meeting ☐ Other:		☐ YES ☐ NO	
		☐ Call ☐ Email ☐ Note ☐ Meeting ☐ Other:		☐ YES ☐ NO	

Observations

Date :

Date :

Date :

Date :

Date :

Date :

Date :

Date :

Date :

Observations

Date :
....
....
....
....
....
....
....
....

Date :
....
....
....
....
....
....
....
....

Date :
....
....
....
....
....
....
....
....

Date :
....
....
....
....
....
....
....
....

Date :
....
....
....
....
....
....
....
....

Date :
....
....
....
....
....
....
....
....

Date :
....
....
....
....
....
....
....
....

Date :
....
....
....
....
....
....
....
....

Date :
....
....
....
....
....
....
....
....

▶▶▶ Student's Name ◀◀◀

ID .... Grade ....

Number

Student info

Student's Name		Student ID	
Date Of Birth		Grade	
IEP Expiration Date		ETR Expiration Date	

ꙮ Contact Info ꙮ

Name		Name	
Relationship		Relationship	
Phone Number		Phone Number	
Email		Email	

ꙮ IEP GOALS ꙮ

ꙮ Related Services ꙮ	Time
☐ Occupational Therapy	
☐ Physical Therapy	
☐ Speech Therapy	
☐ Behavioral Therapy	
☐ Other :	

ꙮ Important Information ꙮ	
Medication	Other

IEP Snapshot

Student's Name: [   ]   Case Manager: [   ]   Date of IEP: [   ]

Disability: [   ]   Eligibility: [   ]   Behavior Plan: [ ] Yes [ ] No

❯ Subject ❯	❯ Goal ❯

❯ Accommodations ❯

IN THE CLASSROOM	TESTING

❯ Strengths ❯	❯ Need To Know ❯

❯ Weaknesses ❯	❯ Notes ❯

IEP Meeting Checklist

Student's Name		IEP Due Date	
Date Of Birth		Classification	
Grade		Meeting Date	

⌄ Before Meeting ⌄

⌄ Day of Meeting ⌄

⌄ After Meeting ⌄

IEP Meeting Notes

Student's Name		IEP Due Date	
Date Of Birth		Classification	
Grade		Meeting Date	

Attendees
- [ ] Parent/Guardian
- [ ] Classroom Teacher
- [ ] Other
- [ ] OT
- [ ] Speech
- [ ] PT

Meeting Purpose
....
....
....

Parent Concerns

Student's Progress

Next Steps

▸▸▸ Progress Monitoring

Progress Monitoring

Student's Name : .... Grade : ....

Goals			
1		2	
3		4	
5		6	

Goal #	Date	Trial 1	Date	Trial 2	Date	Trial 3

⌄ Comments ⌄

Progress Monitoring

Student's Name : ....

Grade : ....

Goals			
1		2	
3		4	
5		6	

Goal #	Date	Trial 1	Date	Trial 2	Date	Trial 3

❤ Comments ❤

Small Group Progress
Monitoring

Subject : .... Week of : ....

Date	Target Skill and Activity	Students	Notes

Communication Log

MOTHER		FATHER		OTHER CONTACT	
Email		Email		Email	
Cell		Cell		Cell	
Work		Work		Work	

DATE & TIME	TO	METHOD OF CONTACT	REASON FOR CONTACT	FOLLOW UP	NOTES
		☐ Call ☐ Email ☐ Note ☐ Meeting ☐ Other:		☐ YES ☐ NO	
		☐ Call ☐ Email ☐ Note ☐ Meeting ☐ Other:		☐ YES ☐ NO	
		☐ Call ☐ Email ☐ Note ☐ Meeting ☐ Other:		☐ YES ☐ NO	
		☐ Call ☐ Email ☐ Note ☐ Meeting ☐ Other:		☐ YES ☐ NO	
		☐ Call ☐ Email ☐ Note ☐ Meeting ☐ Other:		☐ YES ☐ NO	
		☐ Call ☐ Email ☐ Note ☐ Meeting ☐ Other:		☐ YES ☐ NO	

Communication Log

DATE & TIME	TO	METHOD OF CONTACT	REASON FOR CONTACT	FOLLOW UP	NOTES
		☐ Call ☐ Email ☐ Note ☐ Meeting ☐ Other:		☐ YES ☐ NO	
		☐ Call ☐ Email ☐ Note ☐ Meeting ☐ Other:		☐ YES ☐ NO	
		☐ Call ☐ Email ☐ Note ☐ Meeting ☐ Other:		☐ YES ☐ NO	
		☐ Call ☐ Email ☐ Note ☐ Meeting ☐ Other:		☐ YES ☐ NO	
		☐ Call ☐ Email ☐ Note ☐ Meeting ☐ Other:		☐ YES ☐ NO	
		☐ Call ☐ Email ☐ Note ☐ Meeting ☐ Other:		☐ YES ☐ NO	
		☐ Call ☐ Email ☐ Note ☐ Meeting ☐ Other:		☐ YES ☐ NO	
		☐ Call ☐ Email ☐ Note ☐ Meeting ☐ Other:		☐ YES ☐ NO	

Observations

Date :

Date :

Date :

Date :

Date :

Date :

Date :

Date :

Date :

Observations

Date :

Date :

Date :

Date :

Date :

Date :

Date :

Date :

Date :

▶▶▶ Student's Name ◀◀◀

┌─────────────────────────────────┐
│   │
│   │
│   │
└─────────────────────────────────┘

ID ....   Grade ....

Number

┌──────────┐
│   │
│   │
└──────────┘

Student info

Student's Name		Student ID	
Date Of Birth		Grade	
IEP Expiration Date		ETR Expiration Date	

ⱱ Contact Info ⱱ

Name		Name	
Relationship		Relationship	
Phone Number		Phone Number	
Email		Email	

ⱱ IEP GOALS ⱱ

ⱱ Related Services ⱱ	Time
☐ Occupational Therapy	
☐ Physical Therapy	
☐ Speech Therapy	
☐ Behavioral Therapy	
☐ Other :	

ⱱ Important Information ⱱ	
Medication	Other

IEP Snapshot

Student's Name: _____ Case Manager: _____ Date of IEP: _____

Disability: _____ Eligibility: _____ Behavior Plan: ☐ **Yes** ☐ **No**

❯ Subject ❮	❯ Goal ❮

❯Accommodations❮

IN THE CLASSROOM	TESTING

❯ Strengths ❮	❯ Need To Know ❮

❯Weaknesses❮	❯ Notes ❮

IEP Meeting Checklist

Student's Name		IEP Due Date	
Date Of Birth		Classification	
Grade		Meeting Date	

⌄ Before Meeting ⌄

⌄ Day of Meeting ⌄

⌄ After Meeting ⌄

IEP Meeting Notes

Student's Name		**IEP Due Date**	
Date Of Birth		**Classification**	
Grade		**Meeting Date**	

Attendees ☐ Parent/Guardian   ☐ OT   ☐ PT

☐ Classroom Teacher   ☐ Speech

☐ Other

Meeting Purpose
....
....
....

❤ Parent Concerns ❤

❤ Student's Progress ❤

❤ Next Steps ❤

▶▶▶ Progress Monitoring

Progress Monitoring

Student's Name : .... Grade : ....

Goals			
1		2	
3		4	
5		6	

Goal #	Date	Trial 1	Date	Trial 2	Date	Trial 3

ⱽ Comments ⱽ

Progress Monitoring

Student's Name : .... Grade : ....

Goals			
1		**2**	
3		**4**	
5		**6**	

Goal #	Date	Trial 1	Date	Trial 2	Date	Trial 3

˅ Comments ˅

Small Group Progress
Monitoring

Subject : .... Week of : ....

Date	Target Skill and Activity	Students	Notes

>>> Communication Log <<<

MOTHER	FATHER	OTHER CONTACT
Email	Email	Email
Cell	Cell	Cell
Work	Work	Work

DATE & TIME	TO	METHOD OF CONTACT	REASON FOR CONTACT	FOLLOW UP	NOTES
		☐ Call ☐ Email ☐ Note ☐ Meeting ☐ Other:		☐ YES ☐ NO	
		☐ Call ☐ Email ☐ Note ☐ Meeting ☐ Other:		☐ YES ☐ NO	
		☐ Call ☐ Email ☐ Note ☐ Meeting ☐ Other:		☐ YES ☐ NO	
		☐ Call ☐ Email ☐ Note ☐ Meeting ☐ Other:		☐ YES ☐ NO	
		☐ Call ☐ Email ☐ Note ☐ Meeting ☐ Other:		☐ YES ☐ NO	
		☐ Call ☐ Email ☐ Note ☐ Meeting ☐ Other:		☐ YES ☐ NO	

Communication Log

DATE & TIME	TO	METHOD OF CONTACT	REASON FOR CONTACT	FOLLOW UP	NOTES
		☐ Call ☐ Email ☐ Note ☐ Meeting ☐ Other:		☐ YES ☐ NO	
		☐ Call ☐ Email ☐ Note ☐ Meeting ☐ Other:		☐ YES ☐ NO	
		☐ Call ☐ Email ☐ Note ☐ Meeting ☐ Other:		☐ YES ☐ NO	
		☐ Call ☐ Email ☐ Note ☐ Meeting ☐ Other:		☐ YES ☐ NO	
		☐ Call ☐ Email ☐ Note ☐ Meeting ☐ Other:		☐ YES ☐ NO	
		☐ Call ☐ Email ☐ Note ☐ Meeting ☐ Other:		☐ YES ☐ NO	
		☐ Call ☐ Email ☐ Note ☐ Meeting ☐ Other:		☐ YES ☐ NO	
		☐ Call ☐ Email ☐ Note ☐ Meeting ☐ Other:		☐ YES ☐ NO	

Observations

Date :

Date :

Date :

Date :

Date :

Date :

Date :

Date :

Date :

Observations

Date :

Date :

Date :

Date :

Date :

Date :

Date :

Date :

Date :

▶▶▶ Student's Name ◀◀◀

ID .... Grade ....

Number

Student info

Student's Name		Student ID	
Date Of Birth		Grade	
IEP Expiration Date		ETR Expiration Date	

⅋ Contact Info ⅋

Name		Name	
Relationship		Relationship	
Phone Number		Phone Number	
Email		Email	

⅋ IEP GOALS ⅋

⅋ Related Services ⅋	Time
☐ Occupational Therapy	
☐ Physical Therapy	
☐ Speech Therapy	
☐ Behavioral Therapy	
☐ Other :	

⅋ Important Information ⅋	
Medication	Other

IEP Snapshot

Student's Name: [ ] Case Manager: [ ] Date of IEP: [ ]

Disability: [ ] Eligibility: [ ] Behavior Plan: [ ] **Yes** [ ] **No**

ⅴ Subject ⅴ	ⅴ Goal ⅴ

ⅴ Accommodations ⅴ

IN THE CLASSROOM	TESTING

ⅴ Strengths ⅴ	ⅴ Need To Know ⅴ

ⅴ Weaknesses ⅴ	ⅴ Notes ⅴ

IEP Meeting Checklist

Student's Name		IEP Due Date	
Date Of Birth		Classification	
Grade		Meeting Date	

⌄ Before Meeting ⌄

⌄ Day of Meeting ⌄

⌄ After Meeting ⌄

IEP Meeting Notes

Student's Name		**IEP Due Date**	
Date Of Birth		**Classification**	
Grade		**Meeting Date**	

Attendees
☐ Parent/Guardian ☐ OT ☐ PT
☐ Classroom Teacher ☐ Speech
☐ Other

Meeting Purpose
....
....
....

❧ Parent Concerns ❧

❧ Student's Progress ❧

❧ Next Steps ❧

▶▶▶ Progress Monitoring

Progress Monitoring

Student's Name : .... Grade : ....

Goals			
1		2	
3		4	
5		6	

Goal #	Date	Trial 1	Date	Trial 2	Date	Trial 3

⌄ Comments ⌄

Progress Monitoring

Student's Name : ....   Grade : ....

Goals	
1	2
3	4
5	6

Goal #	Date	Trial 1	Date	Trial 2	Date	Trial 3

Comments

Small Group Progress
Monitoring

Subject : ....   Week of : ....

Date	Target Skill and Activity	Students	Notes

Communication Log

MOTHER		FATHER		OTHER CONTACT	
Email		Email		Email	
Cell		Cell		Cell	
Work		Work		Work	

DATE & TIME	TO	METHOD OF CONTACT	REASON FOR CONTACT	FOLLOW UP	NOTES
		☐ Call ☐ Email ☐ Note ☐ Meeting ☐ Other:		☐ YES ☐ NO	
		☐ Call ☐ Email ☐ Note ☐ Meeting ☐ Other:		☐ YES ☐ NO	
		☐ Call ☐ Email ☐ Note ☐ Meeting ☐ Other:		☐ YES ☐ NO	
		☐ Call ☐ Email ☐ Note ☐ Meeting ☐ Other:		☐ YES ☐ NO	
		☐ Call ☐ Email ☐ Note ☐ Meeting ☐ Other:		☐ YES ☐ NO	
		☐ Call ☐ Email ☐ Note ☐ Meeting ☐ Other:		☐ YES ☐ NO	

>>> Communication Log <<<

DATE & TIME	TO	METHOD OF CONTACT	REASON FOR CONTACT	FOLLOW UP	NOTES
		☐ Call ☐ Email ☐ Note ☐ Meeting ☐ Other:		☐ YES ☐ NO	
		☐ Call ☐ Email ☐ Note ☐ Meeting ☐ Other:		☐ YES ☐ NO	
		☐ Call ☐ Email ☐ Note ☐ Meeting ☐ Other:		☐ YES ☐ NO	
		☐ Call ☐ Email ☐ Note ☐ Meeting ☐ Other:		☐ YES ☐ NO	
		☐ Call ☐ Email ☐ Note ☐ Meeting ☐ Other:		☐ YES ☐ NO	
		☐ Call ☐ Email ☐ Note ☐ Meeting ☐ Other:		☐ YES ☐ NO	
		☐ Call ☐ Email ☐ Note ☐ Meeting ☐ Other:		☐ YES ☐ NO	
		☐ Call ☐ Email ☐ Note ☐ Meeting ☐ Other:		☐ YES ☐ NO	

Observations

Date : ....

....
....
....
....
....
....

Date : ....

....
....
....
....
....
....

Date : ....

....
....
....
....
....
....

Date : ....

....
....
....
....
....
....

Date : ....

....
....
....
....
....
....

Date : ....

....
....
....
....
....
....

Date : ....

....
....
....
....
....
....

Date : ....

....
....
....
....
....
....

Date : ....

....
....
....
....
....
....

Observations

Date :

Date :

Date :

Date :

Date :

Date :

Date :

Date :

Date :

▶▶▶ Student's Name ◀◀◀

ID .... Grade ....

Number

Student info

Student's Name		Student ID	
Date Of Birth		Grade	
IEP Expiration Date		ETR Expiration Date	

♥ Contact Info ♥

Name		Name	
Relationship		Relationship	
Phone Number		Phone Number	
Email		Email	

♥ IEP GOALS ♥

♥ Related Services ♥	Time
☐ Occupational Therapy	
☐ Physical Therapy	
☐ Speech Therapy	
☐ Behavioral Therapy	
☐ Other :	

♥ Important Information ♥

Medication	Other

IEP Snapshot

Student's Name: _____   Case Manager: _____   Date of IEP: _____

Disability: _____   Eligibility: _____   Behavior Plan: ☐ **Yes** ☐ **No**

❤ Subject ❤	❤ Goal ❤

❤ Accommodations ❤

IN THE CLASSROOM	TESTING

❤ Strengths ❤	❤ Need To Know ❤

❤ Weaknesses ❤	❤ Notes ❤

IEP Meeting Checklist

Student's Name		IEP Due Date	
Date Of Birth		Classification	
Grade		Meeting Date	

❤ Before Meeting ❤

❤ Day of Meeting ❤

❤ After Meeting ❤

IEP Meeting Notes

Student's Name		**IEP Due Date**	
Date Of Birth		**Classification**	
Grade		**Meeting Date**	

Attendees
☐ Parent/Guardian ☐ OT ☐ PT
☐ Classroom Teacher ☐ Speech
☐ Other

Meeting Purpose

♥ Parent Concerns ♥

♥ Student's Progress ♥

♥ Next Steps ♥

►►► Progress Monitoring

Progress Monitoring

Student's Name : .... Grade : ....

Goals		
1		2
3		4
5		6

Goal #	Date	Trial 1	Date	Trial 2	Date	Trial 3

˅ Comments ˅

>>> Progress Monitoring <<<

Student's Name : ....   Grade : ....

Goals				
1			**2**	
3			**4**	
5			**6**	

Goal #	Date	Trial 1	Date	Trial 2	Date	Trial 3

❦ Comments ❦

Small Group Progress
Monitoring

Subject : ....

Week of : ....

Date	Target Skill and Activity	Students	Notes

⠶⠶ Communication Log ⠶⠶

MOTHER	FATHER	OTHER CONTACT
Email	Email	Email
Cell	Cell	Cell
Work	Work	Work

DATE & TIME	TO	METHOD OF CONTACT	REASON FOR CONTACT	FOLLOW UP	NOTES
		☐ Call ☐ Email ☐ Note ☐ Meeting ☐ Other:		☐ YES ☐ NO	
		☐ Call ☐ Email ☐ Note ☐ Meeting ☐ Other:		☐ YES ☐ NO	
		☐ Call ☐ Email ☐ Note ☐ Meeting ☐ Other:		☐ YES ☐ NO	
		☐ Call ☐ Email ☐ Note ☐ Meeting ☐ Other:		☐ YES ☐ NO	
		☐ Call ☐ Email ☐ Note ☐ Meeting ☐ Other:		☐ YES ☐ NO	
		☐ Call ☐ Email ☐ Note ☐ Meeting ☐ Other:		☐ YES ☐ NO	

>>> Communication Log <<<

DATE & TIME	TO	METHOD OF CONTACT	REASON FOR CONTACT	FOLLOW UP	NOTES
		☐ Call ☐ Email ☐ Note ☐ Meeting ☐ Other:		☐ YES ☐ NO	
		☐ Call ☐ Email ☐ Note ☐ Meeting ☐ Other:		☐ YES ☐ NO	
		☐ Call ☐ Email ☐ Note ☐ Meeting ☐ Other:		☐ YES ☐ NO	
		☐ Call ☐ Email ☐ Note ☐ Meeting ☐ Other:		☐ YES ☐ NO	
		☐ Call ☐ Email ☐ Note ☐ Meeting ☐ Other:		☐ YES ☐ NO	
		☐ Call ☐ Email ☐ Note ☐ Meeting ☐ Other:		☐ YES ☐ NO	
		☐ Call ☐ Email ☐ Note ☐ Meeting ☐ Other:		☐ YES ☐ NO	
		☐ Call ☐ Email ☐ Note ☐ Meeting ☐ Other:		☐ YES ☐ NO	

Observations

Date :

Date :

Date :

Date :

Date :

Date :

Date :

Date :

Date :

Observations

Date :

Date :

Date :

Date :

Date :

Date :

Date :

Date :

Date :

▶▐▐▶ Notes

Notes

Notes

Notes

Notes

Notes

Notes

Notes

Notes

Notes

Notes

Notes

Notes

Notes

Notes

Notes

Notes

Notes

Notes

Notes

Notes

Notes

Notes

Notes

Notes

Notes

Notes

Notes

Notes

Notes

Notes

Notes

Notes

Notes

Notes

Notes

Notes

Notes

Notes

Notes

Notes

# Notes

Notes

Made in United States
North Haven, CT
06 July 2023

38649844R00198